Herm

A little souvenir

CHRIS ANDREWS
PUBLICATIONS

Herm

Herm lies about three miles to the east of Guernsey. It is only one and a half miles long by three quarters of a mile wide, yet visitors to the island feel that here time itself has been stretched out. Perhaps it is the peacefulness, the calmness, the quiet – the name itself is said to mean "deserted land". Whatever the special quality is, time spent on Herm is to be savoured slowly.

After a series of private tenants, including the writer Compton Mackenzie who also leased Jethou, Herm was purchased from the Crown in 1946 for the sum of £15,000. Leased out to the Wood family by the States of Guernsey since 1949, Herm has been developed in a way that maximizes the Island's resources without impinging on its natural charm and beauty. Dependent for much of its income on tourism, old farm cottages have been renovated to provide holiday accommodation, campsites have been established and amenities provided, and the hotel modernized. Day-trippers are well catered for, as Herm village has shops as well as a tavern and restaurant. There is a working farm, a manor house, the small yet beautiful St. Tugual's chapel, and many delightful walks and beaches.

Herm and Jethou at dawn   5

6   Ferry at Rosaire

Whilst known for many years as the playground for the Governors of Guernsey and their guests, Herm's long history reveals a more important role. It is believed that Herm was originally a burial ground for French kings – prehistoric remains and artefacts unearthed show them to be too many for the size of community that would have existed in Herm. Monks inhabited the island at various periods of its history, as late as the 1880s. Quarrying became important in Herm in the 1830s and there was also a largely unsuccessful copper mine, above Rosaire.

Harbour at high tide   7

Shell Beach with Sark in the distance

10 St Tugual's Chapel

Herm is not just a holiday island. It is very much a community. It has its own school, power station, fire service, chapel and even a prison – one of the smallest in the world. For both residents and visitors alike, Herm, with its beautiful beaches, proliferation of bird life, profusion of wild flowers and general air of calm and well-being, has what Jenny Wood called, a "magical appeal".

The White House Hotel   11

12   Harbour jetty and The White House Hotel from the sea

Ferry and the west coast with the famous Foxgloves   13

14   Harbour over Fisherman's Bay

16 Low tide at the harbour

18 Belvoir Bay with summer flowers

Belvoir Bay and Shell beach   19

20   Shell Beach and the east coast

Shell Beach and offshore rocks 21

22 Shell Beach in the evening

Shell Beach, Alderney Point and Mouisonniere Beach   23

Oyster rock and South along Bears Beach

26 Bear's Beach and the Obelisk

Fisherman's Cottage and Hermetier at early sunset 27

28   Flowers on the hill

30   Cottages in the Harbour Village and The Hotel

The south east, Jethou, and Guernsey's St Martin's Point   31

32   Cottages at Manor Village

34   Luggage delivery, Herm Style

Past cottages at Manor Village, and an old well covered in summer blooms   35

36   Looking back to Guernsey

38   The White House Hotel gardens facing Guernsey

40 Fisherman's Beach leading to the harbour

42   The harbour and village

44   Offshore rocks at the north end and Alderney

View of Sark from Herm   45

46   The Tower at the centre of the Island

48   The Common in autumn

Bracken and grasses stand out against a winter sea and Jethou   49

50   The way back to the harbour

Autumn colours at Fisherman's Beach   51

52   Hermetier and Guernsey from Herm

Herm has abundant flowers, here growing wild on the west coast   53

54   The west coast looking south to Guernsey

The west coast (Fisherman's Beach and cottage) looking north west 55

56 Jethou from Herm on a blustery day

58   A shaft of silvery light in the late afternoon

Cliff path and wild flowers at the south end   59

60   The tiny cemetery above Bear's Beach

Gulls and wild flowers on the cliffs between Belvoir and Shell Beach

62   Late evening sun on the south east cliffs with Sark in the distance

The anchor at Harbour Beach and Jethou   63

Produced for Herm Island

www.herm-island.com +44(0)1481 722377

by

Chris Andrews Publications

Telephone: +44(0)1865 723404 email:chris.andrews1@btclick.com

Photos by Chris Andrews and Herm Island, Text Dallas Masterton.

ISBN 0 954033 183

CN00689654

LÉON BAKST

and the

Art of the Ballets Russes

A BOOK OF POSTCARDS

*San Francisco Performing Arts
Library and Museum*

POMEGRANATE ARTBOOKS, SAN FRANCISCO

Pomegranate Artbooks
Box 808022
Petaluma, CA 94975

ISBN 1-56640-442-8
Pomegranate Catalog No. A649

Pomegranate also publishes over sixty other postcard collections on different subjects.
Please write to the publisher for more information.

Upon completing his formal art study in Paris (1893–1896), Léon Bakst (b. 1866) returned to his native Russia, where he became an organizer of and an active participant in the Mir Iskusstva (World of Art) group. There he met Serge Diaghilev and Alexander Benois, with whom he worked on exhibitions in St. Petersburg and at the Salon d'Automne (Paris, 1906). In 1909 he moved permanently to Paris, arriving some months after Diaghilev and his opera and ballet troupe.

Diaghilev's group soon became known as the Ballets Russes. Bakst immediately was made a member of the core group, along with Diaghilev, Benois and the ballet master Mikhail Fokine. In his first season, Bakst's set designs for *Cleopatra* caused a great sensation; with them began his ever-increasing popularity. Bakst would create more and more of the company's costume and stage designs in the next few seasons. In fact, with Benois's temporary retirement, all productions for the entire 1912 season were de-signed by Bakst.

Although Bakst would become the production director of the Ballets Russes in the years following, less and less of the actual designs and decor would be his. Bakst's movement into the background paralleled that of the group itself, which would never recreate the sensational impact of its first few seasons in Paris. Bakst died in Paris in 1924, and with Diaghilev's death in 1929 the Ballets Russes disbanded.

The illustrations in this book of postcards are reproduced from *The Decorative Art of Léon Bakst* (1913) and are from the peak years of Bakst's work with the Ballets Russes.

LÉON BAKST and the Art of the Ballets Russes
Léon Bakst (1866–1924)
Costume of the "Silver" Negro
From the ballet *Scheherazade,* 1910
Watercolor, gouache and silver paint on paper

Pomegranate, Box 808022, Petaluma, CA 94975

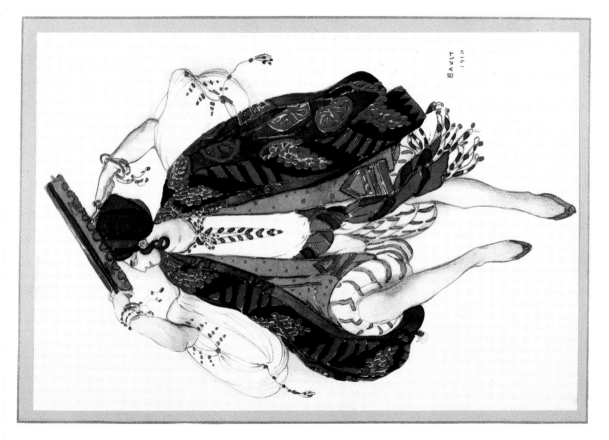

LÉON BAKST and the Art of the Ballets Russes
Léon Bakst (1866–1924)
Costume for the Hebrew Dance
From the ballet *Cleopatra*, 1910
Watercolor, gouache and gold paint on paper

Pomegranate, Box 808022, Petaluma, CA 94975

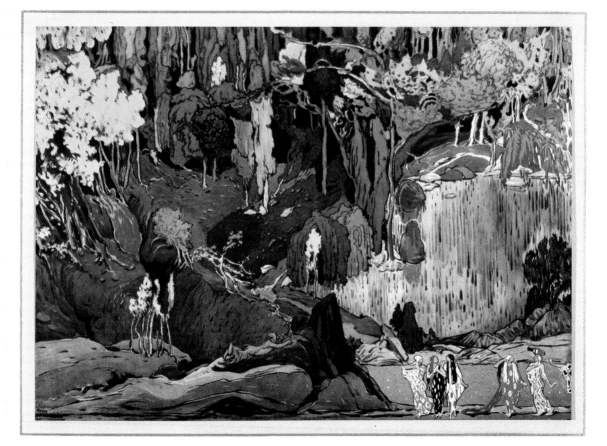

LÉON BAKST and the Art of the Ballets Russes
Léon Bakst (1866–1924)
Set sketch
From the ballet *Afternoon of the Faun,* 1912
Gouache on paper

Pomegranate, Box 808022, Petaluma, CA 94975

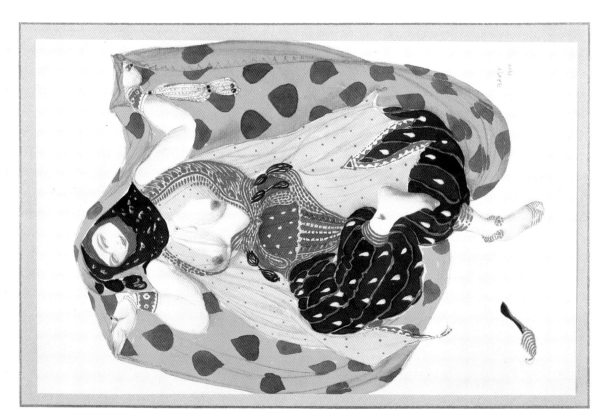

LÉON BAKST and the Art of the Ballets Russes
Léon Bakst (1866–1924)
Costume of an Odalisque
From the ballet *Scheherazade*, 1910
Watercolor and gouache on paper

Pomegranate, Box 808022, Petaluma, CA 94975

LÉON BAKST and the Art of the Ballets Russes
Léon Bakst (1866–1924)
Set sketch
Maquette du Décor du Prologue from *La Pisanelle*
Watercolor on paper

Pomegranate, Box 808022, Petaluma, CA 94975

LÉON BAKST and the Art of the Ballets Russes
Léon Bakst (1866–1924)
Costume of the Red Sultan
From the ballet *Scheherazade,* 1910
Gouache and gold paint on paper

Pomegranate, Box 808022, Petaluma, CA 94975

LÉON BAKST and the Art of the Ballets Russes
Léon Bakst (1866–1924)
Set sketch
From the ballet *Daphnis and Chloe,* 1912
Watercolor and gouache on paper

Pomegranate, Box 808022, Petaluma, CA 94975

LÉON BAKST and the Art of the Ballets Russes
Léon Bakst (1866–1924)
Costume of the Faun (Nijinsky)
From the ballet *Afternoon of the Faun*, 1912
Pencil, watercolor, gouache and gold paint on
cardboard

Pomegranate, Box 808022, Petaluma, CA 94975

LÉON BAKST and the Art of the Ballets Russes
Léon Bakst (1866–1924)
Set sketch
From the ballet *Daphnis and Chloe,* 1912
Watercolor on paper

Pomegranate, Box 808022, Petaluma, CA 94975

"DIEU BLEU"
(un jeune)

BAKST
1911

LÉON BAKST and the Art of the Ballets Russes
Léon Bakst (1866–1924)
Costume of the Blue God
From the ballet *The Blue God,* 1911
Watercolor, gouache and gold paint on paper

Pomegranate, Box 808022, Petaluma, CA 94975

LÉON BAKST and the Art of the Ballets Russes
Léon Bakst (1866–1924)
Set sketch
From the ballet *Le Secret du Harem,* n.d.
(not staged)
Oil on canvas board

Pomegranate, Box 808022, Petaluma, CA 94975

LÉON BAKST and the Art of the Ballets Russes
Léon Bakst (1866–1924)
Costume of Iskander (Nijinsky)
From the ballet *La Peri*, 1911
Watercolor, gouache and gold paint on paper

Pomegranate, Box 808022, Petaluma, CA 94975

LÉON BAKST and the Art of the Ballets Russes
Léon Bakst (1866–1924)
Set sketch
From the ballet *Thamar*, 1912
Watercolor and gouache on paper

Pomegranate, Box 808022, Petaluma, CA 94975

LÉON BAKST and the Art of the Ballets Russes
Léon Bakst (1866–1924)
Costume of the Pilgrim
From the ballet *The Blue God,* 1911
Watercolor and gouache on paper

Pomegranate, Box 808022, Petaluma, CA 94975

LÉON BAKST and the Art of the Ballets Russes
Léon Bakst (1866–1924)
Set sketch
From the ballet *Scheherazade*, 1910
Watercolor, gouache and gold paint on paper

Pomegranate, Box 808022, Petaluma, CA 94975

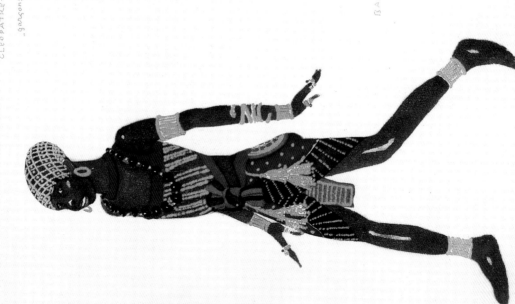

CLÉOPATRE.
"garçons-arabes"

BAKST
1910

LÉON BAKST and the Art of the Ballets Russes
Léon Bakst (1866–1924)
Costume for a Negro youth
From the ballet *Cleopatra,* 1910
Watercolor, gouache and silver paint on paper

Pomegranate, Box 808022, Petaluma, CA 94975

des Costumes de "SHÉHÉRAZADE"

Aquarelles Originales   de Léon Bakst

LÉON BAKST and the Art of the Ballets Russes
Léon Bakst (1866–1924)
Various costumes
From the ballet *Scheherazade*, 1910
Pencil, watercolor, gouache and gold paint on
paper

Pomegranate, Box 808022, Petaluma, CA 94975

LÉON BAKST and the Art of the Ballets Russes
Léon Bakst (1866–1924)
Costumes of Beotian women
From the ballet *Narcissus*, 1911
Pencil, watercolor, gouache, gold and silver
paint on paper

Pomegranate, Box 808022, Petaluma, CA 94975

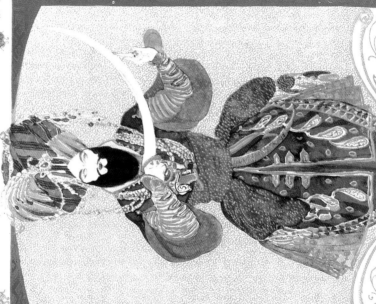

LES BALLETS RUSSES

SUPPLÉMENT AU N° DU 15 JUIN 1910 DE.

COMŒDIA ILLUSTRÉ

NUMÉRO SPÉCIAL CONSACRÉ A LA SAISON RUSSE

NUMÉRO SPÉCIAL CONSACRÉ A LA SAISON RUSSE

A L'OPÉRA BALLETS

BALLETS

1910

SAISON RUSSE

LÉON BAKST and the Art of the Ballets Russes
Léon Bakst (1866–1924)
Ballets Russes program cover, June 1910
Watercolor, gouache and gold paint on paper

Pomegranate, Box 808022, Petaluma, CA 94975

LÉON BAKST and the Art of the Ballets Russes
Léon Bakst (1866–1924)
Costume of a Beotian
From the ballet *Narcissus*, 1911
Pencil, watercolor and gouache on paper

Pomegranate, Box 808022, Petaluma, CA 94975

LÉON BAKST and the Art of the Ballets Russes
Léon Bakst (1866–1924)
Set sketch
From the ballet *The Blue God,* 1911
Watercolor and gouache on paper

Pomegranate, Box 808022, Petaluma, CA 94975

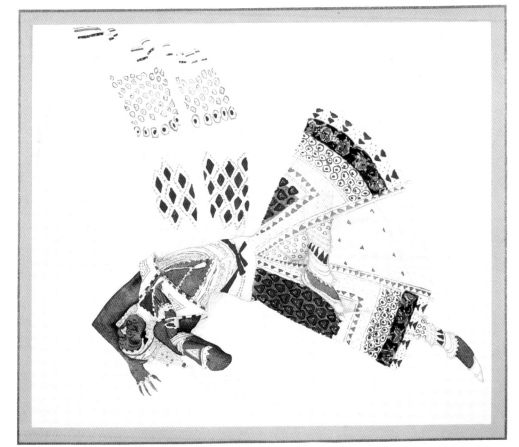

LÉON BAKST and the Art of the Ballets Russes
Léon Bakst (1866–1924)
Costume of a young Beotian
From the ballet *Narcissus*, 1911
Watercolor, pencil and gold paint on paper

Pomegranate, Box 808022, Petaluma, CA 94975

LÉON BAKST and the Art of the Ballets Russes
Léon Bakst (1866–1924)
Set sketch
From the ballet *Narcissus*, 1911
Watercolor and gouache on paper

Pomegranate, Box 808022, Petaluma, CA 94975

"NARCISSE"
Demi-Divinité
(Aquarelle de Léon BAKST)

LÉON BAKST and the Art of the Ballets Russes
Léon Bakst (1866–1924)
Costume of Bayadere
From the ballet *The Blue God,* 1911
Pencil and watercolor on paper

Pomegranate, Box 808022, Petaluma, CA 94975

LÉON BAKST and the Art of the Ballets Russes
Léon Bakst (1866–1924)
Set sketch
From the ballet *Helen of Sparta*, 1912
(not staged)
Watercolor and gouache on paper

Pomegranate, Box 808022, Petaluma, CA 94975

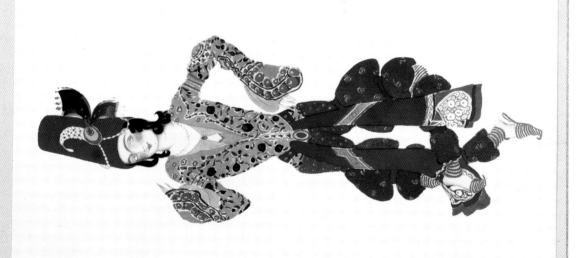

LÉON BAKST and the Art of the Ballets Russes
Léon Bakst (1866–1924)
Costume of an Indian youth
From the ballet *Scheherazade,* 1910
Watercolor, gouache and gold paint on paper

Pomegranate, Box 808022, Petaluma, CA 94975

LÉON BAKST and the Art of the Ballets Russes
Léon Bakst (1866–1924)
Set sketch
From the ballet *Daphnis and Chloe,* 1912
Watercolor on paper

Pomegranate, Box 808022, Petaluma, CA 94975

LÉON BAKST and the Art of the Ballets Russes
Léon Bakst (1866–1924)
A demigod
From the ballet *Narcissus*, 1911
Pencil and watercolor on paper

Pomegranate, Box 808022, Petaluma, CA 94975

LÉON BAKST and the Art of the Ballets Russes
Léon Bakst (1866–1924)
Ballets Russes program cover, 1909
Watercolor, gouache and gold paint on paper

Pomegranate, Box 808022, Petaluma, CA 94975